BUSINESS IN THE BLUE

Helpful Tips To Stay Successful When Depression Hits

Ivy N. McQuain

Business In The Blue

Helpful Tips To Stay Successful When Depression Hits

Ivy N. McQuain

Published by

BLI Publishing, LLC
P.O. Box. 1931
Cedar Hill, Texas 75104
469-557-1254
www.blipublishing.com

Printed by KDP Amazon

Printed in the United States of America

Designed by BLI Publishing, LLC

ISBN: 978-0-9988802-1-1

This book is dedicated to every business owner, entrepreneur and professional who struggles to make it through another day because of their battle with depression. My hope is that this book will allow you to see the brighter side of things.

This book is also dedicated to my classmate Sonja Johnson Pierre. You were a light unto this world that ended too soon. The Peabody Magnet High School in Alexandria, Louisiana Class of 1997 misses you.

Acknowledgments

Thank you to everyone who listened to me during moments when I couldn't stand the sound of my own voice because I was fed up with being a business owner. You know who you are.

Thank you to my sons, Dee and Nick. The two best people who I never hope to ever fail. You two young men are amazing and I thank God He chose me.

Thank you mom, you rock lady.

Table of Contents

Introduction

There were many days when getting out of the bed was one of the hardest thing to do. I mean literally trying to decide if it was worth the effort to get up, sit down in front of my computer, and create or execute the plan that was beneficial to my life. Entrepreneurship and business ownership are not only rewarding but are also lonely, difficult, and full of setbacks. The reasons for the vast hurdles are unlimited. From client issues, plans not working out the way you thought, to personal issues including financial, sickness, and family. That's why so many business owners and entrepreneurs are left sitting on the edge of the ledge wondering if pushing forward another day in business is worth it.

But it is.

It is so worth it when you are able to be in charge of your life and running the business you love on your terms. This is the reason I wrote this book, Business in the Blue: Ensuring Your Business Survives When Depression Hits, to help you fight depression while trying to successfully grow your business and thrive at it.

Depression is often defined as having an extended period of sadness. But if you have ever had an all out fight with depression, then you know it's more than sadness. It can and is oftentimes overwhelmingly crippling and life changing. You feel as if there is nothing that you can do right as it relates to your clients, making money moves, and growing or sustaining your business. Even when everything is on the right track and successful. Depression convinces you that you are nothing more than just an insignificant little no one and you will never impact the world or your industry.

Here's something to always remember. You are successful despite how you feel and despite what your mind is trying to convince you of. You are going to win against your battle against depression. You are going to win at growing your business. You are going to win at life and be everything you believe and know that you are. You have to speak life into yourself every day, even when it doesn't matter. There is no question about it. Even if you have to write affirmations to yourself and place them all over the place. You have to know that you will win against depression and your business will be successful.

I can go on and on and I will as we move through

this book to help you understand that depression is not a permanent stop in your life. It's very temporary. Yes, it's a rollercoaster ride that can and will impact your business. This book will hopefully help you to move around the roadblocks that depression causes to help you win in your business, to win overall, and become a kick ass business owner.

Let's dive in!

(Disclaimer: I am not a medical or healthcare professional. The writings in this book are from my personal experiences. If you are experiencing depression or severe depression with suicidal thoughts then please go get help.)

Depression and You

Some studies suggest that depression is a hereditary mental condition or illness. According to the article Is Depression Hereditary? By Michael J. Meaney Ph.D. on September 3, 2015 on Psychology Today website, "Depression runs in families, which implies the influence of particular genes that may render an individual vulnerable to the illness. Very often families with mental or behavioral disorders are also families in which there exists a considerable amount of dysfunction." Though there is no true scientific data that outright identifies the link between depression and familial genetics, it is very plausible that there is a link.

However, there are other reasons as to why depression hits.

As mentioned before, depression can pause your life when you have difficulty from a client, when your payments start to arrive late or not at all, and when your business takes an unexpected or unplanned downturn. You may find it difficult to fully recover from. Again, this is not a full list of reasons but it can start from one of these points and develop into something more serious. Depression has so many physical attributes and can literally kill your business and can even kill you. Thankfully there are many remedies such as counseling, medication regimen, holistic methods, and most importantly prayer. Let me say this, prayer without works (getting the help that you needs) does not work.

So why am I writing this book? Yes, there are millions of books out there talking about depression and how to push through it. Well this book is different, sort of. My goal is to talk about depression as it relates to being a business owner and how to push through and still win in business when depression cripples your life. Remember when I mentioned that depression can be triggered from things like clients, bad deals, and just your business getting away from you? Well, those are real life situations that have caused many business owners to pack it up and quit. Some never look back at entrepreneurship.

Depression has impacted my life more than I care to recall. Matter of fact in 2016 I was severely depressed and in the fall of 2017 as well as the first quarter of 2018. Did my business suffer? Does a squirrel likes acorns? Of course, my business suffered. I went from earning six-figures in 2017 to making standard wages in 2018. My overall health was one of the reasons caused many other health issues. Nonetheless all of these setbacks spawned several bouts with depression.

Fortunately, I learned how to finally put my business on autopilot so it could run when I wasn't able to get out of the bed. That is what I want to share with you in this book. How to save your business while you battle depression.

Are you ready to win when depression hits?

Of course you are.

Chapter 1

Let's talk about what may have caused your depression

Everyone lives with, suffers from, and battles depression differently. There are baseline identifiers to help you understand what may have triggered your depression. To be honest, it is different for everyone. Depression, just like any other illness, mental or physical, affects everyone on various levels. For instance, a loss of something important may cause someone to slip into a depression - where they spend all their time. While someone else may suppress and isolate themselves to keep from being reminding of any familiarity of what they loss. Yet in still, someone else a mourn to the point of death. It's all relative and different for each person living with some form of depression.

The one thing that is the same across the board is that depression is very real and it really does affect the individual's life on a level that can ultimately and negatively impact their business.

There are things in your life that can make you beyond sad. What is beyond sad? It is the inability to shake the feeling of just being sad. You know like watching a movie where the guy doesn't get the girl. That's sad. Your depression may cause you to not only feel sad about the guy not getting the girl but feel like you'll never find the perfect relationship or that your relationship is a wreck even though your partner does everything possible to make you happy. Beyond sad suffocates you and makes you feel worthless in every aspect of your life, even when you are winning at life and in business. Beyond sad (depression) will cost you many good and valuable relationships.

I remember when I was married, my ex was a great guy, even though I was a spoiled, my way or the highway, control freak. My ex went to work, never cheated, loved our boys, and did whatever he could to make it work. Unfortunately, I was so consumed with "being me" that I would become crippled by depression. So much so that I contemplated suicide when I felt that things were not going my way.

My triggers were simple at best, such as my sons being unruly, my husband not making six figures, or slow paying clients. Mind you they were between the toddlers and elementary age. I wanted everything my way and when it didn't I allowed depression to take a hold of me. If I couldn't go on a shopping spree because of poor saving habits and budgeting habits, then I got depressed. If I couldn't talk to the people I wanted to talk to because they were busy, then I would slip into depression and wanted to end relationships. If my clients demanded too much of me, then I felt inadequate and became depressed.

My depression, though it sounds temperamental, was very real. I was accustomed to making things work when I wanted it to work. I started my life as an adult at a very early age. So all I knew was making it happen for myself.

So the simple things that I couldn't control became the triggers of my life. The things that I thought that I had figured out and that made sense to me eventually crippled my business and kept me from functioning at times. Even to this day there are moments when depression sets in and I shrink inside of myself. My business tends to suffers overwhelmed and look for help I don't have at times. I get drained from having to be a beast all of the time.

Quick Exercise

So what are affects you and causes you to go into depression? List three things that you know for a fact that will make you beyond sad.

Don't give too much description right now. The next few lessons will do that. I just want you to get an idea of what triggers your depression. Identifying at least the base root of your depression will help you gain insight as to how you can keep pushing forward in your business when depression hits. There is hope… let's find it together.

Use the next four pages to write your thoughts out.

1. What makes me sad?

_____

_____

_____

_____

_____

_____

_____

_____

_____

_____

_____

_____

_____

_____

_____

_____

_____

_____

_____

_____

_____

_____

_____

2. What makes me sad?

_____
_____
_____
_____
_____
_____
_____
_____
_____
_____
_____
_____
_____
_____
_____
_____
_____
_____
_____
_____
_____
_____
_____
_____
_____
_____

3. What makes me sad?

Overflow Thoughts

_____
_____
_____
_____
_____
_____
_____
_____
_____
_____
_____
_____
_____
_____
_____
_____
_____
_____
_____
_____
_____
_____
_____
_____

Chapter 2

Knowing what depression means to you

Depression is the elephant in the room that we try to ignore. You know how people say let's address the elephant in the room but no one really does, so he stays right there hidden in plain sight? That's depression. The thing that many people don't know how to address or talk about because they think that depression is simply a temper tantrum or sadness. Depression is what depression is but sadness can feel like depression.

I am being honest because not getting my way and losing control of my environment sent me into depression many times. It has cost me wonderful relationships because I changed who I was when I was depressed. It affected my sons tremendously, even into their adult lives. I can't tell you the hell I caused in my marriage because I lost control and couldn't make things happen the way that I wanted it to happen. I was a mover and shaker and when I got married I had to give that up to cater to him. I thought that you could have it all but my reality was that if you want a happy husband who is willing to do everything for you and the family without cheating and feeling like he doesn't matter then you have to actually be a wife first. I wasn't a wife. I was a businesswoman first and his wife when I finished handling business. Needless to say I am divorced.

Yet in still, I can go on and on but we all know that when we lose control of our environment because of depression it hurts more than just us. In my opinion depression looks like a temper tantrum minus laying on the floor kicking and screaming. Instead we withdraw and go deep into our "safe place" that is usually dark and lonely. We swear no one understands us and that the world would be better without our presence.

I am a living testimony of this! I had to make adult decisions at a very early age. Depression became my escape. It became a reason for me to "act the way I acted." An excuse to have a crappy attitude because I didn't want to be without the people in my life. Depression became a drug for me because it allowed me to avoid accepting the reality that sometimes you lose control and it's okay. It was my dark place... my sunken place minus the crazy white family trying to kill me. Depression is not always an emotion that keeps you slumped in the corner wishing for death.

Sometimes it's acting out. Some may now call it bipolar disorder but it may actually be just good old depression rearing its ugly head in some shape or form.

One of the best ways to truly understand what depression is to identify what depression is to you and how it affects your every day life. Identify three things that your depression does for you. If you have more great but let's focus on small bits first.

Quick Exercise:

This exercise is to help you really get a grasp of what depression means to you. Some people don't think that they live or suffer from depression because they identify it as something else that others go through that makes them crazy. Trust me the more you deny your feelings, the more you will continually have setbacks and your business will continue to suffer.

1. Depression to me is...

_____
_____
_____
_____
_____
_____
_____
_____
_____
_____
_____
_____
_____
_____
_____
_____
_____
_____
_____
_____
_____
_____
_____
_____
_____

2. Depression to me is...

_____
_____
_____
_____
_____
_____
_____
_____
_____
_____
_____
_____
_____
_____
_____
_____
_____
_____
_____
_____
_____
_____
_____
_____
_____
_____

3. Depression to me is...

Overflow Thoughts

Chapter 3

How depression has affected your life and business

Now that we are moving along with understanding you and your depression let's get into how it affects your life and your business. Again, depression can be crippling. It can cause your life to go into a complete tailspin. It happens. But the best part of depression is learning everything you can about YOUR depression because YOUR depression is specific to YOU! The common misconception is that depression is cookie cutter. There is a such thing as functioning while depressed. It doesn't mean that your depression is not real or less severe as someone who never leaves the house. It just mean that you may not be fully coping with your level of depression.

During my depressive episodes I often stop working or become sluggish. I miss personal business deadlines during my depression and my goals become extended without an end date. I become a resolutioner. You know the person who faithfully sets New Year's resolutions to accomplish without end dates? I get away from my to do lists and rely on my memory, which can become focused on everything else. I watch more television or stare off into the abyss.

Depression can extremely affect your life and your business. Hell it can affect your career if you don't have a business. It can make you wonder, 'why the hell am I getting out of bed.' It can make you look at world through a dark glass and wonder why the sun isn't shining. Depression is what it is and it is what it's mean to be... darkness. Regardless if it's functioning or not depression has one job and that is to utterly destroy your life.

Quick Story:

I remember one of my lengthy bouts with depression when I refused to take on new clients. I had a rough patch with a client. Mind you I am a full time business owner so for me not to want to take on new clients meant I should just pack it up and get a job. I was beat down and wanted nothing to do with another so-called business person who was just as janky as Ice Cube's character in Janky Promoters. I honestly didn't care where I was going to get money from as long as I didn't have to interact with other people. I was done and depression was winning. So I started writing again as a freelance writer which wasn't paying any bills. But it was giving me money here and there and that was more than I wanted. My bills got behind because my depression crippled me and fear set in thinking about dealing with people.

Not only was I depressed but I also had anxiety. Talk about a horrible combination. I was a mess. And this lasted not days or weeks but months. Thank God He always put a ram in the bush and money came without much effort from me so that forced me to work. If my livelihood had to depend solely on me at that time, then I would be under a bridge begging for coins because I had given up.

Quick Exercise:

Regardless of what you think, depression has and will continue to hurt your business. So be honest with yourself with this exercise and identify the top three times how depression has hurt your business and what happened when you got depressed.

You can't move past depression if you are not willing to identify it. Everyone is different.

1. How has depression hurt my business and what happened?

---

2. How has depression hurt my business and what happened?

_____
_____
_____
_____
_____
_____
_____
_____
_____
_____
_____
_____
_____
_____
_____
_____
_____
_____
_____
_____
_____
_____
_____
_____

3. How has depression hurt my business and what happened?

_____
_____
_____
_____
_____
_____
_____
_____
_____
_____
_____
_____
_____
_____
_____
_____
_____
_____
_____
_____
_____
_____
_____
_____

Overflow Thoughts

_____
_____
_____
_____
_____
_____
_____
_____
_____
_____
_____
_____
_____
_____
_____
_____
_____
_____
_____
_____
_____
_____
_____
_____
_____

Chapter 4

Identify the people who contribute to your depression

Clients. Employees. Family. Friends.

When you own a business the lines easily become blurred. You can easily start to think and believe that everyone is out to sabotage you or you will start to sabotage your relationships for a chance at peace. Healthy relationships are the most important thing in the world to have. But the most important relationship to have is the one with yourself.

- If you have the personality of someone who jumps in the fire for everyone, then you are doomed and you will live depression every time they no longer need you.
- If you have the personality of someone who is codependent, then depression is a space that you will live when they pull away.
- If you have the personality of someone who

prefers to be alone, then depression is a space that you will live because you're alone.

- If you have the personality of someone who has to win all the time no matter what, then depression is a space that you will live in when you lose.

- If you have the personality of someone who is outgoing and the life of the party, then depression is a space that you will live when you're invites stop coming.

I think you get the point. No matter your personality depression can and will hit, winning or not, outgoing or not. It does not care who you are and what you portray yourself to be. One of the things that can and will impact your so-called personality is who you surround yourself with.

Yes, the people who you give your time to will either bring you out of depression or push you further into depression. These people will also have a powerful impact on your business as a whole.

For instance if you have children, a spouse, friends, or even family who are always full of drama and are needy (after a certain age for your children of course) then your time will be focused on them and the attention you give your business will dwindle. You will start neglecting the things you need to do and your revenue will start to suffer. Or like me you will neglect your home life, children and spouse, and then your business will still dwindle because now you have a mess that you have to clean up at home. Either way you are screwed and depression will be waiting to attack if you don't get things under control.

When I was married one of the things I struggled with was dividing my attention. I fought my depression by focusing on work. I didn't know my sons' school schedule, my husband's work hours or anything. I lived my life according to my client's need and when they didn't pay their invoice, it affected my emotions and my household. My life was business because I started my first business at 19 to take care of myself and my oldest son, while in college. Business was my personality. It was my way of life and when I didn't have it I was off balanced emotionally. I didn't feel validated unless I was talking business or making a business deal or working on something business related. But I was never giving 100 percent towards neither my business or my family because depression was holding a 40 percent stake in my life.

Not only was my personal life in shambles but I was always willing to end a friendship at a moments notice, because depression controlled my thoughts. I would literally call my high school friends on a conference call and say that I was done with them. Albeit that I may not have spoken to them in months.

When business went south I was cutting ties with everyone. I was that determined to let my depression and codependency on my business control me.

My external life was hectic. My mother has always been my rock but I was emotionally abusive towards her a times because she didn't have a business, so she couldn't understand my life. Tuh. How foolish! Thank God she has labored with me to understand that depression controlled me most of the time and my thoughts were not mine at times.

Does this sound familiar? Have you lost control in areas of your life that you need to gain control back over? Do you think that it's too far gone? If so, then stop that! That's your depression talking. Everything can be fixed with a conversation and a desire to understand the other person's feelings.

When you have a business you MUST establish an understanding of your limits. Yours and yours alone. I can't speak of balance because that word sends people into a tailspin. Everyone speaks of balance but it's a personal journey and it's not cookie cutter. My definition of balance was waking up a 5 a.m. and either answering my emails, or being on social media until 9 a.m. or reading my Bible and praying. Or I might be going back to sleep. But it was my method of getting ready for my day. So understanding your limits is for you. It helps you from plummeting into a full out depressive state of being. It is a little bit of what you like to do and what may make you uneasy. Meditating and prayer makes me uneasy because I have to slow my mind down and focus on one thing.

Let's look at what you can do to better understand your limits:

- Take personal time of 30 minutes up to two hours. YES, I said up to two hours. Once you start to balance out your diet then you will be able to get the gunk out of you body that contributes to your inability to sleep on a healthy schedule. Everyone has 30 minutes and honestly they have more than two hours. We just choose not to utilize those hours. Depression has proven that we have all the time in the world. When depression hits we have cried for more than two hours, or slept or stared off into space. So take the time to set your first limit and that's personal time.

- Let your mind drift off with a journal and pen in your hand. As a writer and publisher one of the hardest things for me to do is record my feelings when I feel good. I got it covered with recording my sadness but when I feel good I forget about everything. When you sit and think about what you are going through, take the time to get a true sense of what are you feeling. Write it down so when you start to feel sad you can go back to those days to remember every day is not a sad day.

- Surround yourself with people you don't know. Being around your circle can add to your depressive state because they "know" you, they may not understand your level of depression, and they may need something from you. You need the peace of strangers. Go to the local bookstore, mall, or wherever there are strangers who may not offer conversation and who you can watch. Sometimes watching others can help you see the beauty in living. This is one of my favorite things to do when I hit a low point in my life, people watching. I get laughs, shocks, and the ability to be nosey.

Quick Exercise:

It's hard to take an honest look at the people aroudn you and see that they are your stressors that lead you to depression. After all you believe you are responsible for their well being and that is a lot to take on. But guess what? You're really not responsible for them unless you are their parent and even then there is an age limit on taking care of them. You can't take care of everyone and not yourself.

Look around your life and take inventory of those people around you who add to your depression. Write their names out and what they do that brings you down, then write down what you are going to do to change that to stay away from depression. If you have more than three then you may have a bigger people than you realize.

1. This person _____
aids in my depression. So what am I going to do
about it?

----

1. This person _____
aids in my depression. So what am I going to do
about it?

----

1. This person _____
aids in my depression. So what am I going to do
about it?

_____
_____
_____
_____
_____
_____
_____
_____
_____
_____
_____
_____
_____
_____
_____
_____
_____
_____
_____
_____
_____
_____
_____

Overflow Thoughts

Chapter 5

How money can affect your depression

I know there have been many days when clients have felt that paying their invoice is not a priority or a necessity especially around birthdays, holidays, and other significant days in their personal lives. It is enough to make you want to scream and holler, cry and beg, and then want to fight. Not getting the money you need is the one thing that sends many business owners into depression. The inability to get invoices paid hinders success and stops the ability have a debt-free and worry-free business life.

But it doesn't always have to be like that.

Quick Story:

I remember it vividly. I had one client, whom I admired, who started me on a long path in depression. This client had several important dates that superseded my invoices. With that being said the money owed went unpaid, therefore, rent went unpaid; followed by an eviction notice; followed by an eviction. I sent emails pleading for my money but my client's personal life was much more important. I various motels with my sons from July to December, when the next large contract closed.

My entire income is based on if a client decides to pay or not. Talk about dealing with long bouts of depression. You work hard to get the client, to make them happy, to do the best work possible, then boom they decide not to pay you. I have so many stories like this and so many instances of being depressed and not wanting to work anymore, especially as an entrepreneur.

Yeah, it's easy to say, 'Go get a job!' but when God places something inside of you, you realize that He will always make a way. That six months in the motels taught me a couple of things: living in motels ain't really that bad and to never depend on a limited stream of income. I did because I trusted my work ethics and my ability to deliver the very best. Thank God that situation helped me to wake up to do better.

Do I still fumble with clients? Yes, because I still hold myself to a standard when it comes to doing what's right.

How can you make sure that you minimize or eliminate monetary issues with clients? You need to, not should, have an automated system in place to make sure that your payments come even when you don't feel like asking for your money. I know I hate chasing my money and sometimes I won't even bother because it honestly gets old having to constantly ask for my money when my services have been rendered. People always say they have bookkeeping practices on their end as if I am sitting idly counting change. I assure you that I am not. But I also assure you that it hurts having to beg for my money or to remind clients to pay their invoices.

The systems I use allows me automate payment reminders for my clients. I have the app on my phone for on the go needs. This is why it is important to collect their banking or credit card information so that you can set up an auto draft payment system. All you need to do is send a credit/debit card payment agreement and make sure they return it before the contract is signed. If they pay their regular bills on time, then they can pay you on time. If they don't, then you will be in trouble. And please don't tell me that PayPal is the only money mangement system that you have. PayPal is no longer the best.

Evaluate your prices for your services or products. My rule of thumb is that your prices should completely cover your bills. You need to have one or two kick ass products or services that are going to take care of you when you can't take care of yourself. That doesn't mean raise your services/products to the point of impossible affordability. No, it simply means that you need to evaluate what you have and adjust. This also means that you need to adjust it accordingly. If you are a go-getter, then your clients need to reflect just that. If you have a tendency to rush and be last minute, then guess what so shall your clients be? It's all relative and you are who you attract.

You should also have products that can sell even when you are sleeping. That may include instruction manuals, books, t-shirts, pre-recorded tutorials, etc. Something that moves even when you can't. These types of products should be thoughtfully planned and easy to produce when you have minimum energy to do the work.

Another thing you need to do is to make sure that you have a business account set up for your business and only use it for business. Nothing more frustrating than spending your business money for you personal needs including rent, lights, or eating out. Unless it is a legitamite business expense, don't use your business account. You should have a DBA (Doing Business As) bank account set up for your business needs only. I can't tell you how many times I have used money out of my business account for something that should be in my personal account. Research or talk to a Certified Public Accountant or bookkeeper on how you should use your business account if you are unsure.

Quick Exercise:

This exercise is a little more detailed because you now have to look at your money management systems, products/services, and when you need to implement thse items to help you stay afloat when you can't get out of the bed.

Let's look your money management systems. What are the fees per transaction. Can you invoice your clients? What about on the go?

1. _____

_____

_____

2. _____

_____

_____

3. _____

_____

_____

What are your top three products/services and each price point? How can you adjust each to make sure they are automated when you can't operate?

1. _____
_____
_____
_____
_____

2. _____
_____
_____
_____
_____

3. _____
_____
_____
_____
_____
_____
_____

Now list some new products/services that you want to create that will generate income without you.

1. _____
_____
_____
_____
_____
_____
_____

2. _____
_____
_____
_____
_____

3. _____
_____
_____
_____
_____
_____
_____

So when do you need to accomplish these things? NOW! While you feel strong enough to get things done.

Overflow Thoughts

Chapter 6

Be willing to manage your depression

I know seeing the header makes you say, "You clearly don't deal with depression."

Trust me, I do but I also know that you have to have the will power for mental fortitude to get out of your head and get back into the game. Other than that you are going to end your business and the relationships you have built. I have lost business and relationships for being that person while depressed. I made mistake after mistake. So much so I took any client, even the ones I knew were toxic because I allowed my depression to impact my earnings.

Quick Story:

There's one client who sticks out the most for me that threw me into a deep depression for almost a year. I went from a six figure income to almost half of that the following year. I didn't want to take on new clients because I didn't want to deal with a devil in disguise like my previous client. I didn't want to negotiate a lower rate like I allowed for this previous client. I just didn't. And believe me when I say it had a very adverse impact on my well-being and my financial freedom. I think I spent more time in bed watching television than I did since I was a child.

As I look back I am glad that I did because it helped me come up with the concept of this book and it definitely helped me to realize that I needed some kind of system in place in order to make sure that my business ran smoothly whether I was involved or not. That's hard to do for many entrepreneurs or small business owners. This particular client had such a negative impact on my health and was a monster clothed in Jesus scriptures. Just horrible. And the worst part that, I think most business owners can agree on, was her refusal to take ownership of any wrongdoing.

Nonetheless, I was still in control of my emotions and how I handled the depression that I allowed myself to go into. I refused to get help when I found myself slipping into the abyss. I refused to handle the situation as I needed to. I definitely refused to shake it off and move forward. I just laid in the bed knowing I needed to make money but refusing to earn it because I just didn't.

My depression was all on me and getting out of it when I noticed the signs was something I failed to do. An entire year passed by with me being the victim of familiar circumstances. I allowed my bad judgement to place me in a horrible situation that I knew what was going to happen from the start. Let me tell you this… when a potential client asks for a discount, especially if there is a prior relationship there, then consider that they may not be the best customer for you. Your prices are your prices. Always remember that. **NO DISCOUNTS!**

I forgot that and that was how that particular client triggered my depression. It cost me more money than I have ever lost. That 'need more' drug over took me and I made bad decisions all year just to deal with the late payments and stress from having to keep my composure with one client. Oh… what's the 'need more' drug? It's the constant need for more especially when you don't have money or opportunities presented to you as you should or once had.

I said all of that to say at some point you should know when you are being triggered into depression. It doesn't just come out of the blue like a thief waiting in a dark alley. No it is not. There are things that happen to trigger your sadness, moodiness, or loneliness. That is why it is important for you to be aware of your triggers, to record them in a journal, and talk to your mental health professional. If you don't, then everything that comes your way is a possible hindrance to your business. I know what avoiding my issues causes. I have gone one too many days without making an earning, looking for clients, and hurting relationships. It is on you to be an advocate for yourself and your business.

Quick Exercise:

You can manage your depression but you have to be more than willing to manage your depresssion. It makes no sense to be this great business person who lives in a constant state of depression when there are things around you that you can do to literally help you get out of your own way.

1. Identify some ways that you can use to push yourself when you feel the onset of depression.

_____
_____
_____
_____
_____
_____
_____
_____
_____
_____
_____
_____
_____
_____
_____
_____
_____
_____
_____
_____
_____
_____
_____
_____
_____

2. Identify some ways that you can use to push yourself when you feel the onset of depression.

_____
_____
_____
_____
_____
_____
_____
_____
_____
_____
_____
_____
_____
_____
_____
_____
_____
_____
_____
_____
_____
_____
_____
_____
_____
_____

3. Identify some ways that you can use to push yourself when you feel the onset of depression.

Overflow Thoughts

_____
_____
_____
_____
_____
_____
_____
_____
_____
_____
_____
_____
_____
_____
_____
_____
_____
_____
_____
_____
_____
_____
_____
_____
_____
_____

Chapter 7

Encourage or curse yourself out

I am a true advocate of cursing myself out, especially when I can't seem to get out of bed because I am depressed. I talk to myself like I don't know me. No, it's not crazy because I have weighed my friends down with my up and down emotional rollercoaster and my clients don't need to know that part of me. So I tell myself to get up and continue to be the best business representative for my business. It's up to me and it all depends on me to be what my clients need and what my business needs.

When you are an entrepreneur the only person you have to motivate you IS YOU. So what happens when you fall into depression? Your business suffers! It's that simple. Your clients have paid you for a service or product within a certain timeframe they honestly don't care about when you are upset or depressed. Their business depends on your delivery. That means you have to encourage yourself or curse yourself out to get going.

There's no easy way to say it. Either convince yourself to get out of the bed or pull yourself up with some harsh words and make it happen. If you had to go to work every day, then guess what you'd take your butt to work and make it happen to get that paycheck. Being an entrepreneur is no different. You have to go and get that money or you are not going to be able to pay your rent, lights, or whatever else. You can't afford the depression.

You are not crazy when you encourage or curse yourself out to get going. What you are is determined to live your life without depression holding you down. If you need help, then call that one friend who is not afraid to dig in your ass to make you move. That person who is sympathetic to your depressive episodes but not willing to allow you to go into the black hole of depression. Let me be clear, you have to that person first before you can ever go out and find another person who can help you. Your business needs you to be tough in the streets and tough internally with yourself when you find that you are not living up to your own standards.

Quick Story:

With my most recent bout with depression I had made up in my mind that I no longer wanted to do the business that I was doing and was looking for something new. I laid around acting as if I had no bills that were continually coming through. I started to tap into my savings accounts and other stashed money just to survive. Guess what? I was okay with it because I was unable to function on any level because depression had a strong hold on me. Eventually I started to get calls from my sons and they were needing help financially. I couldn't help.

Do you know what I did? I cursed myself out. Not just for me but for my sons because they didn't deserve a mother who was going to continually give up on herself and her business when things didn't go her way. I used harsh words with myself and those words didn't involve me not wanting to live and me being a failure. No they were words like, "Get your ass outta this bed!" "How are you going to give up on your kids like that?" "You know damn well you deserve a better life than this!" "What's going to happen when your savings run out?"

I even called myself names, but understand that I can handle it. If you were called abusive names, then don't push yourself that hard. You need to find the happy medium to ensure that you are tough with yourself but not to the point that it pushes you towards suicide because it reminds you of past abusive situations from your past.

I also place affirmations around my house and on my computer to ensure that I see that I am worth the effort to keep fighting. That my business is worth having me as its leader. Nothing around me can be successful unless I am successful. That's it. There is nothing more to say about it. You have to know your worth and use that to fight depression.

If you are constantly fighting depression, then you have to go see someone to help you!

Quick Exercise:

Remember you have to encourage or curse yourself out! And trust you can toggle between the two when you need it. The most important thing is that you cannot allow depression to leave you hanging in the wind and not having a solution for what you are going to do about your business.

1. Identify and create some words or phrases that you can use to encourage yourself when you feel depression setting in.

_____

_____

_____

_____

_____

_____

_____

_____

_____

_____

_____

_____

_____

_____

_____

_____

_____

_____

_____

_____

_____

_____

_____

_____

_____

2. Identify and create some words or phrases that you can use to encourage yourself when you feel depression setting in.

_____

_____

_____

_____

_____

_____

_____

_____

_____

_____

_____

_____

_____

_____

_____

_____

_____

_____

_____

_____

_____

_____

_____

_____

3. Identify and create some words or phrases that you can use to encourage yourself when you feel depression setting in.

_____

_____

_____

_____

_____

_____

_____

_____

_____

_____

_____

_____

_____

_____

_____

_____

_____

_____

_____

_____

_____

_____

_____

_____

_____

Overflow Thoughts

_____
_____
_____
_____
_____
_____
_____
_____
_____
_____
_____
_____
_____
_____
_____
_____
_____
_____
_____
_____
_____
_____
_____
_____
_____
_____
_____

Chapter 8

Create a team for your depression

Everyone needs someone. No man or woman is an island. Blah, blah, blah. We know all of the infamous sayings that tell us that we need someone in our corner, especially during our hard times. But it's hard to believe that when we are depressed. Why? Because depression makes you feel like a burden and the first thing someone should tell you when you say, "I feel like a burden," is "You're NOT!"

That doesn't really comprehend when we're entrenched in the belief that our lives are worthless.

When you feel like you're always depressed you start to think that people maybe talking about you because it's a heavy weight for you to carry so you really start to believe it. It's hard to pick up the phone and call people or text someone time after time and say, "I need you." So you start to isolate yourself more and more. You put on a fake smile and pretend once again that everything is okay.

I mean really how many ways can you tell people that you battle depression before they tune you out or think that you are seeking attention? I look at people like Robin Williams, Kate Spade, and Anthony Bouldin who all were the life of the party, if you will, and who all committed suicide because of their depression. They had a team of people around them but I'm sure that at some point they got tuned out and started to believe that they were a burden.

Don't be like them. If you have thoughts of suicide you need to get help immediately. Don't just pray it away. GET HELP. Don't take more antidepressants or stop taking your medicine. GET HELP. I can't stress this enough. There are suicide hotlines you can call if you just feel like people around you have blocked you out.

I have three beautiful friends who I love and who will not only encourage me but curse me out like I pulled out in front of them without my signal on. Ebony, Naami, and Orah. All of these ladies have given me the business and all have added to my journeys through depression on their terms.

- Ebony is my always enduring encourager. She always has a word of love because she has known me for over 25 years. She gives what she needs to give and adds when she needs to. She will call until I answer my phone. I know she will will me back to sanity by reminding me of my passion, business.

- Naami is a mental health professional and knows the whole scenario of depression but she also knows me. She will blah blah blah me to death because she knows that depression can be a temporary journey. So when I need her she will curse me out and threaten me. She's only like 5'3" so it's kinda scary.
- Orah is big sister. She doesn't play. She is a combination of Ebony and Naami. She encourages me while telling me to get my life together before she comes snatch me out of the bed. Again, scary.

These ladies are the definition of love to me and it's important to allow friends like this to encourage you the way they need to in order for you to get out of your depressive funk and get back to the business of your business.

They know two things… I don't want to be someone's employee and I suck as an employee. They also know who I am as a person and that depression does not define me. If you are truly honest you do have a friend or two like this? You may ran them off when you were depressed. Remember I told you that when I went into depression I cut everyone off. It's time to reengage those relationships, if you can, and let them in and create a support system. If you're lucky then they maybe able to help you when you need them to help you with your business.

My friends help me a lot when I am depressed. They have specific duties that I have asked them to do when I can't do anything. I don't call on them much but if I needed them they have access to everything necessary.

You have to build your circle personally and professionally.

I now manage my depression so I don't lose focus on my business. I reach out to my business accountability partner (B.A.P.), I turn on the tunes to get energized to work, I read a motivational book, and I take a look at something in my industry that makes me want to step up my game. I answer the emails I don't want to answer instead of letting them linger. I handle the difficult clients who are being irrational and demanding then I decompress by talking to my B.A.P. I handle things immediately instead of letting it build up and then internally exploding which only hurts me and my reputation.

Let me explain.

Depression can steal your life so in order to combat

it contact your B.A.P. Make sure that you are at least trying to do something. If he/she are a hard ass, then they will make sure you get it done with no excuses. Your B.A.P. should be someone in your industry and who is successful. They need to have listening skills because I have had some business accountability partners who only sought to destroy me and push me down further into depression. Stay away from these people. They are usually depressed and want company. No you don't need someone who is always willing to stroke your hair and tell you great things. You honestly need a kick in the butt to get going. You just need to make sure the B.A.P. you are trusting isn't depressed either. Trust me you can tell.

I strongly recommend that your business relationships stay just that... business. As an entrepreneur you should always consider each relationship. Blurring business relationships can create strife and have a down the line impact that you may regret. If you are blessed that a business relationship blossoms then great but be careful and take it slow. I am the queen of oversharing with my clients and that always caused me problems at some point that I regretted because my depression superseded my ability to deliver.

You should develop a relationship with a business accountability partner (B.A.P.). Someone who will check on you to make sure you are on track with your business goals. Someone who will also make sure you don't deliver excuse after excuse. A business accountability partner is a great way to keep you going when you feel like staying in the bed watching television all day and night avoiding making your business.

One thing to remember is to NOT overburden your B. A. P. with your personal woes. It's easy to do so but let's be honest, that's why you need to build your team of friends who can help you when the going gets tough. That is definitely why you need to have a licensed therapist, mental health coach, or psychologist. Basically someone other than your B. A. P. who is there to help you keep your mind on track for your business.

I want you to seriously ask yourself, who's on my team when I need them? You'd be surprise that sometimes it's not your best friend and it doesn't always have to be. Sometimes it's not your pastor and it doesn't always have to be. Sometimes it needs to be a medical professional like a therapist or psychologist who will listen to you and help you get to the root cause of your depression. It can be a local or an online support group where you take time to talk to people who are going through what you are going through.

Matter of fact, it needs to be other people so you

can give your people a chance to breath. If you're always helping and that spawns your depression then I suggest you change your habits. You are an enabler to some of the people around you and that's no good. Honestly, that's partly your fault especially when you feel unappreciated. That makes you feel depressed. I know this all too well. I went to a therapist after several personal life choices that were just stupid. It was a healthy start to getting back on track. I had best friends who I could talk to but we were all young and trying to find our own way. We all knew that we needed to pray. That is not a bad thing… matter of fact that is the one thing I recommend but my beliefs are a little different than most and very biblical indeed.

Quick Exercise:

Who do you have around you that you can trust? And don't say no one because I assure you during one of your depression battles you cut off your circle because you were thinking of a way to end it all. You have people. Find them and lock them in. You don't have to talk to them every day but they should be aware that you will call on them when you need them. Please don't be the person who only calls when you need someone. That in and of itself causes contention with people and soon they stop answering your calls.

1. Write out three people who can call on. One from your personal life and two business accountability partners. Why are they important to you?

_____

_____

_____

_____

_____

_____

_____

_____

_____

_____

_____

_____

_____

_____

_____

_____

_____

_____

_____

_____

_____

_____

_____

_____

2. Write out three people who can call on. One from your personal life and two business accountability partners. Why are they important to you?

_____

_____

_____

_____

_____

_____

_____

_____

_____

_____

_____

_____

_____

_____

_____

_____

_____

_____

_____

_____

_____

_____

_____

3. Write out three people who can call on. One from your personal life and two business accountability partners. Why are they important to you?

_____

_____

_____

_____

_____

_____

_____

_____

_____

_____

_____

_____

_____

_____

_____

_____

_____

_____

_____

_____

_____

_____

_____

_____

Overflow Thoughts

Chapter 9

Fix your business and your depression

When you have allowed your depression to successfully run your business into the ground, then what? What do you do now that you have allowed your unwillingness to get the work done?

I tell you what you should do. Keep pushing forward or find another way.

One of my authors, Coach D. said his grandmother told him as a youth that you either make a way or make an excuse. Those are truly words to live by. If you have spent too much time in your depression that it is hurting your business then it maybe time for you to just rebrand your business. There is nothing wrong with scaling back your business model or coming up with a totally new plan for business in general. You have the power to control what it is that you need to do to be successful in business but more importantly your personal life.

I have started at least six businesses since I was 19. They all were the same vein of media and marketing but they all had different scopes of work. I hurt a couple of those businesses because my depression almost took me out. Others it was just time to make a change. All in all it's okay to change direction when you no longer see where you belong in your business field.

But how do you fix your business if you don't want to stay the course?

You should seek the help of a mentor who can help you realign your focus. You also need a team and you need someone who will hold you accountable when you feel like giving up. When you are ready get them on the phone or meet them face to face so they can do more than speak a couple of grand words and then check back with you.

Getting back on track should also include you focusing on one major project to complete and set several soft deadlines so that you won't get back into the same boat with depression. If you can't focus on one project then consider outsourcing other projects that will help you focus on what you need to that only you can do. Remember, never put yourself in a position that you can only do what your clients need. Life comes hard and strong and you need to make sure that you can duplicate yourself through outsourcing. Just remember to have agreements in place so that your client confidential information remain intact and your business continues to grow.

Talk honestly with your clients without losing them. That can be hard because your clients wants results. They don't care about your personal life because they too have personal lives but they work their business regardless. You don't have to go into every detail and cry a river but they need to know when you are taking a break and how long you estimate it will be. You can also ask for extensions if you have a deadline driven business but do not make it a habit to make excuses for your depression, especially if you keep letting it control you.

Sometimes our depression is triggered because we don't have a system in place to help with the load of being an entrepreneur/business owner. Relying on the income from others versus the income from working for others can be a tough pill to swallow, especially when payments slow down or stop altogether. That's why it's important to automate your business. You have to have automated systems in place such as invoicing systems with automatic draft, legal documents to sue when clients stop paying or breach their contracts, scheduling software, social media posts scheduling and so much more. While you are on the road to feeling better, your business still needs to operate as if you are still 100 percent in the game.

Here are some great tools:

- Fivver is one of the best tools you can ever use. There are so many creative individuals on the site that you can hire for a small fee. If you are consistent you can build a relationship with them so that you know you will have keep the rhythm to your business.
- Hootsuite is a good site to use for your social media posting. You can create your posts in an excel or .cvs document and mass upload. This helps you remain ahead of the curve when you need to take a break. Hootsuite has a free option as well as a paid option. You can also assign team members to schedule posts.
- Wave is a great invoicing system that has cheaper fees than PayPal. It allows you the option to invoice clients including setting up recurring invoices so you don't miss a beat. You can also perform bookkeeping tasks and a shopping cart you can attach to your website. I all connects to your bank account so you can get paid while you get better.
- Canva helps you create designs through already created templates. Many of their templates are free to use while others you have to pay for. These are great for social

media postings but you can use others for emails and print.

- MailChimp is for email campaigns and newsletters. I love MailChimp because you do so much with it now since its inception. They also have a free option which is great when your clients forget that you have a life to live as well.
- Echo Sign is another great tool to have for business automation because you are able to create and sign documents from your bed on one of those blah days.
- Dropbox and Google Drive are a must so you can store and share important documents with your team.

These are just a few options and YES there are far more than this available. But the point is that you need to get a system in place so you can stay in the game when you have mentally and emotionally checked out of the game because of your depression.

Always remember, it is human nature for clients to strategize their bills in the order of importance. If you are a baker, then that custom cake they want for their event might just become something homemade or store bought. If you are a boutique owner, then those great clothes you have might get replaced with the thrift store finds or something out of the closet. Regardless of your industry, not everyone will see your value no matter how good you are. But if you automate your system then your clients have no reason to forget you when it's time to pay your bills.

Quick Exercises:

Pick the areas that must be operational in your business that need to be automated then find no less than 5 software programs that will help you keep your business running. I say five because you have at least 5 facets to your business:

1. Marketing/Advertising/Promotions
2. Accounting/Bookkeeping
3. Products/Service Development
4. Customer Service
5. Customer Development/Retention

Your turn:

1. _____
2. _____
3. _____
4. _____
5. _____

Now determine what areas that require the most attention in your business for when you become depressed and why.

1. _____

_____

_____

_____

_____

_____

2. _____

_____

_____

_____

_____

_____

3. _____

_____

_____

_____

_____

_____

_____

_____

_____

Next find the solutions. Solutions is just another word for task assignment be it free, outsourced, or automated that will keep you going.

1. _____

_____

_____

_____

_____

_____

2. _____

_____

_____

_____

_____

_____

3. _____

_____

_____

_____

_____

_____

_____

_____

Final thing think of other things that you can do to help you get back on track? These are things that you know you can do better for your business, depressed or not.

1. _____

_____

_____

_____

_____

_____

_____

2. _____

_____

_____

_____

_____

_____

_____

3. _____

_____

_____

_____

_____

_____

_____

Overflow Thoughts

_____
_____
_____
_____
_____
_____
_____
_____
_____
_____
_____
_____
_____
_____
_____
_____
_____
_____
_____
_____
_____
_____
_____
_____
_____
_____
_____
_____
_____

Chapter 10

Take a breather

As a business owner or entrepreneur the only thing we know is the hustle. The grind. The get it how you live. If we're not doing it then we'll be back at a nine to five. That is never the goal of anyone who makes the decision to make money on their terms. Unfortunately, many entrepreneurs who hit the world in pursuit of happiness by their definition end up being a high functioning depressive. That simply means that they show up to every event ready to network, always have a meeting to attend, and are seemingly closing deals.

But that high performance is often an attempt to hide that they are truly living one step above suicide or living in an infinite state of depression. The average high performer is usually just one crash away and has to keep moving in order to not think about what's really eating away at them. I was there.

I was at every event. I was always working on

something. I was just the go to person to get it done. There was nothing that I wouldn't do to hide my depression. I was living the "fake it until you make it" life but I was losing the battle with depression. Finally, I crashed and depression took hold and made me have several seats. My depression had gotten so bad I literally lived in a state of bad decisions always looking for a way to continue fronting like I was happy and everything was perfect.

It was horrible. I cried. Fussed. Cried some more. Was extremely late on projects. Prayed on my face with tears. Laid around crying. I was a perfect mess. But to the outside world I had my life together and business was booming. Yet the invoices were late or not paid. Soon the work was slow coming in. And the bills were piling up. That's when it hit me. Showing up meant nothing if the places I was showing up wasn't producing to provide for the lifestyle I needed. I didn't need people to just like me or my work. I needed them to support my business by either referring me to a paying client or becoming a paying client. I did enough free gigs at the cost of my mental sanity.

That's important to remember. People will free or discount you to death if you allow them and then run away when you ask them to pay an invoice.

Quick Story:

I remember one time I worked as a writer with a young lady who owned a magazine. I worked for her for a while and as soon as I asked her for money she cursed me out like I asked her to pay my rent forever. It was an eye opening experience but I didn't learn because I repeated that same mistake several times over the years with the same results, bills not paid, and depression slipping in. I have so many stories of me giving away my work and many more of me going into depression because of my decision to go go go.

That's why it's important to understand that no matter how fast you move around your depression follows you, and if ignored and unchecked it will win. Then you have to wait for your business to recover. You will not be able to attend the event, book your calendar, or close the sale. Business as usual will not exist. You have to know when it's time to say no, turn off the on sign, and take a break.

Let me say this, **"THERE IS NOTHING WRONG WITH TAKING A BREAK."** Whoever came up with the term 'Team No Sleep' is probably living life at a job waiting for the opportunity to quit. Your body and your mind need rest. There is so much scientific evidence that proves this, so Google it. I know that your body needs rest because it will crash if you ignore the signs.

But for the sake of argument, let's take a look at being a former proud member of Team No Sleep and how it affected my body and ultimately my business. First, the average amount of sleep you need every night is 6-8 hours. We all know that you can function with less sleep but are you really functioning properly?

When I was a dedicated team member of the No Sleep Crew I lived on 2-4 hours of sleep or sometimes no sleep at all. I was always working and always looking for a way to get ahead at that moment. I was a mother of young children, had my own business, and was in college full time. All I knew was working. All I wanted to do was work. So much so that most of the time I threw my body into a tailspin because I was not sleeping nor was I eating properly. My mind was a battlefield and there I went into depression. My body sucked and my mind was horrible.

If that sounds familiar, then you already know what it feels like. It should not feel good and you should not love being in a place where you are constantly drained and frustrated. I have seen my clients work themselves into the ground to only become disgusted and bitter. It's hard to deal with because they then think that what I am adding is not of value. That becomes a drain on me and makes me depressed because I have spent my wheels trying to determine what I can do better.

Here's the reality... I am always giving my all to any project but because they don't have personal life and business values they operate their business in the blue.

I have taken several breaks for from business. Some lasted days and some took me back into the workforce because my sons needed a place to live more than I needed the title of being a business owner.

Quick Story:

While I was married I was fortunate to be able to have my business but when we divorced all of the bills became my responsiblity. Talk about a burden. When I went back into the workforce I started out making $9.10/hour with a Bachelors degree in Marketing. I took a two year break from business while I worked my butt off. Yes, I was depressed soooo many days but I knew that the divorce and getting my sons adjusted to a life without dad was more important than me chasing clients for payment. After the long adjustment I was finally able to get back into the life of being an entrepreneur and was able to earn more money and have more freedom. I was still having to take care of all the bills myself but at least I had a different plan of attack.

In recent times, I have protested being a business owner by being more selective of who I take on as a client and how I wanted to deal with them. I have even gone through the process of firing clients because of their performance within my company. Of course, they got mad but I would rather them to be mad than for me to be stressed and depressed because I am not making money.

You have to decide which is more important, your emotional well being or a client who will jump ship when a new deal comes along.

Quick Exercise:

It's time to be honest about needing and taking a break. There are some things that you can do to help you take your mind off of business. Those are the things that contribute to your overall wellness, emotionally and physically.

1. How do you feel when you take a breather from business? Why?

_____
_____
_____
_____
_____
_____
_____
_____
_____
_____
_____
_____
_____
_____
_____
_____
_____
_____
_____
_____
_____
_____
_____
_____
_____
_____
_____

2. What does taking a breather look like for you. Why?

_____

_____

_____

_____

_____

_____

_____

_____

_____

_____

_____

_____

_____

_____

_____

_____

_____

_____

_____

_____

_____

_____

_____

_____

_____

3. Why haven't you taken a breather?

_____

_____

_____

_____

_____

_____

_____

_____

_____

_____

_____

_____

_____

_____

_____

_____

_____

_____

_____

_____

_____

_____

_____

_____

Overflow Thoughts

_____
_____
_____
_____
_____
_____
_____
_____
_____
_____
_____
_____
_____
_____
_____
_____
_____
_____
_____
_____
_____
_____
_____
_____
_____
_____
_____
_____

Chapter 11

How to move forward

You know this is a conversation that you honestly have to have with yourself. No one knows what it will take for you to get out of depression but you. But one thing is for certain is that if you don't get to moving you might as well close down and get on a corner begging for change to survive. I know this sounds harsh but I am a firm believer that you have to kick yourself in the ass a few times so that you can get your life back on track. Depression takes you out of the game without thinking about what business deals you have going on.

I have been there. At one time I took on so many projects that I failed to see a light at the end of the tunnel. So instead of just getting my execution plan together, thinking my way through it or just using a team to help me, I just slipped into depression. Those projects that were already late become projects that just didn't get done at all. You know what that leads to: more stress and less money. It also can lead to a bad reputation for not getting the work done when it needs to be done. You know people talk about what they don't like more than what they do like.

So again whatever you feel will help you get back on track needs to be a discussion with yourself, God, and if you have a therapist – them too. It is not healthy for you to keep living your life on repeat where you go in constant cycles of ups and downs. If you think that it is okay and that's how you find your next level of creativity then you may have another mental illness such as bipolar disorder versus depression. Again, I am not a psychologist or mental health professional, go to one of them to determine that.

Nonetheless, here are some things that I have done to get out of my slump:

1. I stopped taking new clients until I caught up. Did that hurt financially? Of course it did but what better way for me to learn to stop hurting myself than to put myself on a time out? It also helped me get focused and complete the projects that were outstanding. If you keep taking clients, then you are constantly feeding your depression.
2. I stuck to my therapy appointments. You don't have to go to a therapist, especially if you have can't afford it but you need to do something

therapeutic. I painted, went for a pedicure, massage or just went to my garden. I did anything to take my mind off of feeling the crapiness of depression.

3. I stopped feeding my depression. This one sounds crazy but it's not. If you are a person who sleeps a lot when you become depressed then make it a point to stay away from your house so that you are not tempted to get in the bed. Whatever it is that you do in excess when you are depressed force yourself to do the opposite. I do fail some times but the Lord has a way to make you uncomfortable for Him to get His will out.

You have to stay on top of what your business plan and mental health plan. You can't continuously grow your business if you are constantly detouring with depression. TRUST ME. I have missed so many opportunities because I decided to let my depression run my business into the ground. I have missed events, rescheduled meetings, and just disappeared because I didn't want to be a business owner that day.

Quick Exercise:

If you are going to take a stand against your depression, then you need have a plan of action. Most importantly, you need to stick with it. NO EXCEPTIONS. Too many times I have made plans, wrote them out, and didn't do anything about it because I didn't have a real plan in place for my depression. We all fall short when it comes to doing better for our lives but the things we must do when it comes to depression and your business is to keep moving forward.

What are some things that you can do to help you move forward out of your depression? List three things and then stick to it.

1. What can I do to keep my life moving forward when I am depressed?

_____

_____

_____

_____

_____

_____

_____

_____

_____

_____

_____

_____

_____

_____

_____

_____

_____

_____

_____

_____

_____

_____

_____

_____

_____

_____

2. What can I do to keep my business moving forward when I am depressed?

_____

_____

_____

_____

_____

_____

_____

_____

_____

_____

_____

_____

_____

_____

_____

_____

_____

_____

_____

_____

_____

_____

_____

_____

_____

3. What can I do to ensure my systems are properly in place when I get depressed?

_____

_____

_____

_____

_____

_____

_____

_____

_____

_____

_____

_____

_____

_____

_____

_____

_____

_____

_____

_____

_____

_____

_____

_____

_____

Overflow Thoughts

_____
_____
_____
_____
_____
_____
_____
_____
_____
_____
_____
_____
_____
_____
_____
_____
_____
_____
_____
_____
_____
_____
_____
_____
_____

Chapter 12

Final thoughts

I can't make you get the help you need when it comes to steering clear or minimizing your depression. I struggle with it often. I can only share with you the things that I have done and continually do in order to move forward and to make sure my business survives when depression hits. I am not a medical professional but I have seen a couple of them in my lifetime. I choose not to be on medication for my depression because I believe that some of my symptoms are more self inflicted than mental. Yes, you can go into self-inflicted your depression.

You must choose to succeed in business while living with depression. Learn to be open and honest with yourself first and then keep those on your team. Be informed as to what you truly need to continue to be successful in business. After that have a conversation with your clients if you miss deadlines. When push comes to shove put yourself on timeout and stop taking new clients while you get yourself together. Before you do this make sure you have other streams of income. I am not only a publisher but I am also a notary, certified credit consultant, freelance writer, and other things that don't require much time. These opportunities keep the income coming in while managing my life on my terms.

I take my breaks, my way or the Lord's way. Either way He will make me "sat down" so He can replenish my mind and spirit during my depression. I used to fight it but I lost every time. Now I listen to Him. Yes, I still struggle with my selective spiritual hearing but I know the outcome will be the loss of money, clients and time wallowing in my depression. I also know that He will take His spirit of entrepreneurship away from me if I continue to allow the world to affect my trust in Him. I mean He has never failed me and He will never will.

In closing, do your part to keep your business running. Stop thinking that you are not valuable. You need you more than you know. You have to get healthy in order to win. There are so many people who seemed to have it all together, who are now in the graveyard because they refused to properly manage their depression. They refused to take a step back to reevaluate their lives. Sometimes the business that you are in is not for you forever. Sometimes you have to take a turn. I miss being one of the top media professionals but I don't miss what came with that. STRESS and FALSEHOODS. I love what I do but there will be a time when that chapter comes to an end as well.

I'm always ready for what's next even when I'm not ready. I just know I don't like being depressed about my business.

Just like this one.

Take care of yourself and your business will blossom.

BONUS Chapter

What you eat caues depression

It is a known fact that what you put in your body directly contributes to how you feel. I am a living witness. I had to reverse the effects of fatty liver disease because I was eating meat and a lot of fatty foods like it was about to leave the planet Earth. If it was fried or fried I was eating it. Until one day the food I was consuming fought back and I ended up in the emergency room feeling as if I was going to die. I have children and I must say that pain was worse than giving birth. Birth ends once the baby comes out. Liver pain is continous and God knows I don't want my liver to come out. So I stopped eating meat a for almost a year. I had to include some chicken for protein. Long story short I have A LOT of allergies and fake meat ain't even plant based like it states on the package. When my liver was engourged, I was closing in on 270 lbs. Yeah I am only 5'6".

When I changed my diet I immediately changed how I viewed life and wanted to get a lot accomplished. I also started back working on this book and other projects because I had clarity. I slept better and life started to feel better. Unfortunately, living with depression it comes when it comes and sometimes it lasts longer than expected. Fortunately, during my upv time I was able to capitalize on my great feeling and get things done. The diet change definitely helped with how I was able to perceive my life and what I wanted to get done.

I am no where near the 270 but still I am not at my normal body weight either. But off of that… the purpose of this story was to tell you about how eating healthier can help stabilize your mental wellness. I can give statistical data but use your phone to Google it. Heck, if you have Pinterest, you can definitely find it on there. Your body is not designed to do the impossible, and that is take in a lot of fat, sugars, and other impurities. We were designed to be healthy and with all the health risks associated with just eating you definitely have to be careful with what you put in your body. It's a life must these days. If you are a coffee and donut person, then scale back to once a week as a treat. If you have to get amped up on caffeine just to function, then adjust your sleep schedule and maybe cut out things that cause your attention to be linearly focused. Simply put, stop staying up for three days to catch up in busimess because your depression hit.

You have to discipline yourself to take control of your body because if you don't depression will set in. Depression is not just overeating or sleeping all day, you can function while you're depressed. Simply put you can go through life thinking about how you can exit life instead of being at your best all of the time. There were many days when I worked myself into to the bed or into a doctor's office visit routine that cost me hundreds a week. I successfully ran from everything through working and eating unhealthy.

Food is good for you, of course, but it has to truly be good for you and your mental wellness. You definitely can have cheat days and eat something you love. But you have to be strong enough to get back on track. When depression hits resist the urge to run to those things that keep you from getting better, from feeling better and doing better, emotionally and physically. Don't go into that safe haven of depression where your eating gets out of hand.

That is why eating healthy and maintaining a healthy eating plan is important. Notice I didn't use diet because that word alone might trigger you to feel worthless.

One other thing, if alcohol is your vice, my strong suggestion is that you leave it alone completely. Don't go from being an avid drinker to being a social drinker. This is a form of self-medicating as is the need to eat your pain away. Self-medicating through anything that keeps you from functioning as a business owner without an aid is self-destruction, be it slow or fast. If you need anything to make you appear happy or okay then you are not, I repeat, you are NOT OKAY. You are not living your best life. You are not happy like you portray. You are literally faking it until you make and that is not how you should live your life. You need to address what you are going through and face it head on.

I have watched so many television show that depict people who admit that they used some kind of vice such as unhealthy vice that caused their morbid obesity, coupled with enablers, and they were on the brink of dying but they did not care because they wanted to die although they claimed they wanted to change their lives. It's heartbreaking because as a person who lives with depression I know that we are all on the steps of vice paradise where we allow those simple things to completely control our lives.

Quick Exercise:

You have to know what's controlling you on the inside as well as on the outside. Take a look at your food choices and determine how you can get better with how and what you eat. If you choose to eliminate certain foods from your meal plan, then you will definitely feel better.

What are the things that you may overconsume?

1. _____

_____

_____

_____

_____

_____

2. _____

_____

_____

_____

_____

_____

_____

3. _____

_____

_____

_____

_____

_____

_____

Why do you consume these things? Be honest with yourself.

1. _____

_____

_____

_____

_____

_____

2. _____

_____

_____

_____

_____

_____

3. _____

_____

_____

_____

_____

_____

What are the steps you think you can take to stop or decrease your intake?

1. _____

_____

_____

_____

_____

_____

2. _____

_____

_____

_____

_____

_____

3. _____

_____

_____

_____

_____

_____

_____

How will you commit to your consumption reconstruction?

1. _____

_____

_____

_____

_____

_____

_____

2. _____

_____

_____

_____

_____

_____

_____

3. _____

_____

_____

_____

_____

_____

_____

Now change it. Change is not an overnight process. It takes time but in order to combat your depression you have to look inside and clean your insides.

About the author

I am Ivy N. McQuain. I have several college degrees and professional skills that have allowed me to start and grow several businesses, win awards and recognitions, and travel around the country during my 20 years of being an entrepreneur. I am now the owner of BLI Publishing, LLC, a boutique publishing company that services all areas of publishing from conceptualization to media. It has been my dream since I was a young girl to become a published writer/author and I have succeeded so many times.

None of that means anything because during my tenure in the vast and ever growing field of business

I have also allowed my depression to slow or even stop me altogether. I wrote this book because I want business owners and entrepreneurs to have real expectations as to how depression can and will affect their business when it comes and if it is not properly managed. I have seen great people taken out of the game because their depression was not managed properly.

So, here are my credentials. I have a B.S. in Marketing from Southern University (2002), a M.B.A. and a M.P.A. (Public Administration from the University of Phoenix (2008). I reside in the Dallas, TX area by way of Kansas City, KS. I am the mother of two adult sons, Dee and Nick. They are still my motivation.

My final plea is that you get help for depression lasting more than a couple of weeks. Don't let it cripple your business but most importantly your life. It's okay to pause your business when you need to. Just get the help that you need.

Until the next book, take care of yourself.

.